# Portraits

*from*

## HOLLYWOOD'S GOLDEN AGE *of* GLAMOUR

For Muriel, Nadine, Jr., and Kristi

You know who you are

An imprint of The Rowman & Littlefield Publishing Group, Inc.

4501 Forbes Blvd., Ste. 200

Lanham, MD 20706

www.rowman.com

Distributed by NATIONAL BOOK NETWORK

British Library Cataloguing in Publication Information available

Library of Congress Cataloging-in-Publication Data

Names: Slater, Colin, editor. | Hayes, Melissa, writer of added commentary. | Hollywood Photo Archive.

Title: Portraits from Hollywood's golden age of glamour / Colin Slater and the Hollywood Photo Archive ; text by Melissa J. Hayes.

Description: Lanham, MD : Lyons Press, [2019]

Identifiers: LCCN 2019018880| ISBN 9781493033454 (hardcover) | ISBN 9781493033461 (e-book)

Subjects:  LCSH: Motion picture actors and actresses—California—Los Angeles—Portraits.

Classification: LCC PN1998.2 .P66 2019 | DDC 791.4302/80922—dc23 LC record available at https://lccn.loc.gov/2019018880

∞™ The paper used in this publication meets the minimum requirements of American National Standard for Information Sciences—Permanence of Paper for Printed Library Materials, ANSI/NISO Z39.48-1992.

# *Portraits*

### *from*
## HOLLYWOOD'S
## GOLDEN AGE
## *of* GLAMOUR

**COLIN SLATER'S**
HOLLYWOOD PHOTO ARCHIVE

TEXT BY MELISSA J. HAYES

**LYONS PRESS**

Guilford, Connecticut

# Contents

# About the Hollywood Photo Archive

THE HOLLYWOOD PHOTO ARCHIVE IS NOT ONLY a wonderful collection of cinematic history, but it also captures the collective memories of Hollywood. The gunmen, the gallants, the ghosts, and the stars of the big screen are represented in an impressive archive of more than 180,000 pieces.

The collection has been assembled over forty years by Director Colin Slater. In Slater's early days, as he began to learn his craft, it was the great directors—Wilder, Lean, and Welles—who advised him to study and learn from the film stills. Slater went on to own an important public relations agency, The Adventurers, in association with the legendary journalist and film executive, Fred Hift. Together with 500 stringers the company worked on almost every motion picture produced and released in the U.K., gathering stills from the stars and press collateral from the studios. Added with Hift's lifetime of files, the Hollywood Archive was born.

The outstanding archive provides a treasure trove of prints for film buffs; delve in and discover wonderful film stills, celebrity portraits, and heroic stage performances. For more information contact wkdirections@outlook.com.

# Jean Ackerman

Not actually a Hollywood luminary, Jean Ackerman was a star nonetheless, and was known as the "Queen of the Ziegfeld Follies" in the late 1920s and early 1930s, appearing in such musicals as *Rosalie*, *Whoopee!*, *Midnight Frolic*, and *Smiles*. Jean retired from the stage following her marriage to Walter Hirshon in 1931 and became a prominent New York socialite.

# June Allyson

## 1917 ⌘ 2006

Born Eleanor Geissman in the Bronx, Allyson originally wanted to pursue a medical career, and only started working on Broadway as a way of paying her tuition expenses. MGM executives were so impressed with the Gene Kelly–choreographed musical *Best Foot Forward* (1941), in which Allyson starred, that they "bought" the cast as well as the film rights and moved them all to Hollywood. Thus began Allyson's stellar career, one in which she played "Aw, shucks" girl-next-door types, several of them opposite Jimmy Stewart, as his wife. As Ginger Rogers wrote, "She's the girl every man wants to marry and the girl every woman wants as a friend."

# Ursula Andress

1936 ∽ present

Aptly described on her imbd.com page as "the quintessential jet-set Euro starlet," the Swiss-born Andress is perhaps best known as the first Bond girl, appearing in the debut film *Dr. No* (1962), and setting a high bar for Bond girls to follow. (The bikini she wore in the movie sold at auction for nearly $60,000 in 2001.) She notably played the female lead opposite Elvis Presley in *Fun in Acapulco* (1963), and then went on to appear in many other films in the United States and Europe, until her career ebbed around 1980.

# Julie Andrews

## 1935 ∿ present

At age thirteen, the youngest soloist ever to perform in a Royal Command Variety Performance, a 1948 concert at the London Palladium before King George VI and Queen Elizabeth, Julie Andrews may be the most accomplished actress of our time. Mastering a broad spectrum of popular entertainment, from the theater (*My Fair Lady*), to film (*Mary Poppins*), to a voiceover role in the *Shrek* films, she has won an Academy Award, a BAFTA, five Golden Globes, three Grammys, two Emmys, the Screen Actors Guild Life Achievement Award, the Kennedy Center Honors Award, and the Disney Legends Award. In 2000, Andrews was made a Dame by Queen Elizabeth II for services to the performing arts.

# Ann-Margret

1941 ∽ present

One of the most famous sex symbols of the 1960s, and well into the twenty-first century, Swedish actress Ann-Margret came to the United States at age six. She started as a singer in Las Vegas, where she caught the attention of George Burns. She ended up in his holiday show, performing a soft-shoe dance routine with Burns himself. A record deal at RCA followed, along with a film contract at 20th Century Fox. She became a top box-office draw after *Bye Bye Birdie* (1963) and *Viva Las Vegas* (1964), opposite Elvis Presley. She overcame her "sex kitten" typecasting with Oscar-nominated performances in *Carnal Knowledge* (1971) and *Tommy* (1975), and demonstrated her longevity as an object of desire in *Grumpy Old Men* (1993).

# Lauren Bacall

## 1924 ❦ 2014

Known for her sultry voice and sly good looks, Bacall was born Betty Joan Perske in the Bronx in 1924, and began a modeling career in her teenage years, appearing on a *Harper's Bazaar* cover in 1943. The cover caught the attention of director Howard Hawks's wife, who suggested she take a screen test for the film *To Have and Have Not*, which was then in development. After the screen test Hawks offered her a seven-year contract and a part in the film opposite Humphrey Bogart. Thus began a memorable career (and romance with Bogart) that ultimately led to her being designated the twentieth-greatest female star of classic Hollywood cinema by the American Film Institute.

# Carroll Baker

Perhaps the Hollywood "It Girl" of the 1950s and 1960s, Carroll Baker combined the qualities of a serious dramatic actress with sensual beauty, talents she deployed to good effect in such films as *Baby Doll* (1956), for which she received an Academy Award Best Actress nomination, as well as a Golden Globe Newcomer of the Year Award. After starring in the controversial *Something Wild* in 1961, she appeared in several successful Westerns, including *How the West Was Won* (1962) and *Cheyenne Autumn* (1964). The high point of her career was probably *Harlow* (1965), a much-hyped biopic that nevertheless failed commercially. Following a legal dispute with Paramount, she relocated to Italy, where she made horror films, before returning to the United States to play a few supporting roles in the 1980s and 1990s.

# Lucille Ball

## 1911 ∞ 1989

Largely known for her wisecracking physical comedy through various iterations of *The Lucy Show* from the 1950s to the 1970s, even her most devoted fans overlook Lucille Ball's successful early modeling career in New York as Diane Belmont, where she was discovered by Hollywood and propelled into such dramas as *Blood Money* (1933) and *Stage Door* (1937). Her appearance in *Too Many Girls* in 1940 brought her together with Cuban bandleader Desi Arnaz, leading them to a marital and business partnership that lasted nearly twenty years. After forming Desilu Productions in 1950, the couple originated the hit show *I Love Lucy*, and went on to acquire RKO and develop many other successful television properties. Two years after divorcing Arnaz in 1960, Ball became president of Desilu, the only woman at the time to head a major studio.

# Brigitte Bardot

## 1934 ∽ present

Along with Marilyn Monroe perhaps the best-known sex symbol of the 1950s, to say that Brigitte Bardot has led an interesting life would be a wild understatement. After she appeared in the controversial *And God Created Woman* in 1957, no less an intellectual than Simone de Beauvoir declared Bardot the most liberated woman in France. With a pinup's figure, comely looks, and a talent for acting, singing, and dancing, she appeared in forty-seven movies, recorded over sixty songs, and was for ten years the official face of Marianne, symbol of liberty in France. Following her retirement in 1973, she became a noted animal rights activist, and was even more controversial as an outspoken opponent of Islamic immigration in France in the 2000s.

# Anne Baxter

## 1923 ❧ 1985

Overlooked, perhaps, in an era that contained so many outstanding female actresses, Anne Baxter not only had a creative pedigree as the granddaughter of architect Frank Lloyd Wright, but was also classically trained by actress and teacher Maria Ouspenskaya. Baxter won both an Oscar and a Golden Globe Award for her supporting performance in *The Razor's Edge* (1947), an Academy Award for Best Actress in *All About Eve* (1951), and was nominated for a Primetime Emmy Award in 1969 for an Outstanding Single Performance by an Actress in a Leading Role. Had she not died suddenly at the age of sixty-two, her acting résumé would surely not seem so incomplete.

# Ingrid Bergman

## 1915 ∾ 1982

Perhaps no one epitomized the Golden Age of Hollywood more than Ingrid Bergman, the Swedish-German actress who won fame on both sides of the Atlantic. Beginning her career in Europe in the 1930s, her first US role was in *Intermezzo* (1939), followed by well-known turns in *Casablanca* (1942), and Alfred Hitchcock's *Notorious* (1946). After her affair with director Roberto Rossellini, considered scandalous at the time, Bergman made films in Italy for several years. She returned to a U.S. studio with the production of *Anastasia* (1956), for which she earned her second Oscar, one of three she won, along with *Gaslight* (1944) and *Murder on the Orient Express* (1974). Acclaimed for her Nordic beauty and fierce intelligence, the American Film Institute named Bergman the fourth-greatest female screen legend of all time.

# Claire Bloom

## 1931 ❧ present

An English film and stage actress, Claire Bloom and her family lived through the Blitz in World War II London. After studying drama and spending time in the United States, Bloom debuted on the London stage at sixteen. She appeared alongside Richard Burton in *Hamlet*, and in *Romeo and Juliet*, where critic Kenneth Tynan declared her the best Juliet he'd ever seen. Other leading roles followed, in plays like *A Streetcar Named Desire* and *Long Day's Journey into Night*, and in more than sixty films alongside Laurence Olivier, John Gielgud, Yul Brynner, and Paul Newman. Bloom played the role of Queen Mary in *The King's Speech* (2010), and was appointed Commander of the Order of the British Empire (CBE) in 2013, for services to drama.

# Clara Bow

## 1905 ⤚⤙ 1965

Given her difficult childhood, surrounded by violence and poverty in Brooklyn, New York, no one could have predicted that Clara Bow would become the original "It Girl" of the Roaring Twenties. Winning a photo beauty contest led to her appearance in forty-six silent films, and later, eleven talkies, including *Mantrap* (1926), *It* (1927), and *Wings* (1927). Bow was a huge box-office draw; at the height of her popularity, in 1929, she received more than 45,000 fan letters in a single month. Bow wasn't as comfortable with sound films, and at the age of twenty-six, she married fellow actor and cowboy star Rex Bell and retired from acting, moving to Nevada to become a rancher. Film aficionados rediscovering the joys of silent film appreciate her legacy today.

# Louise Brooks

## 1906 ⌘ 1985

Famous for her signature bob, Louise Brooks personifies the flapper of the silent film era. She began her career as a chorus girl in the 1925 *Ziegfeld Follies* on Broadway, attracting the attention of both Charlie Chaplin (with whom she had an affair) and Paramount producer Walter Wanger (who signed her to a five-year contract). Always a rebel, Brooks refused to be restricted by society's rules for women. She went off to Europe and starred in G. W. Pabst's *Pandora's Box* and *Diary of a Lost Girl* in 1929. She was featured in seventeen silent films and eight sound films before she retired in 1938, at the height of her career, generally dissatisfied with Hollywood. Brooks spent her days painting, reading, and writing, until her death at age seventy-eight.

# Claudia Cardinale

## 1938 ⌒ present

When Italian-Tunisian actress Claudia Cardinale won a beauty competition in 1957, the prize was a trip to Italy, which led to film contracts. Known for her portrayal of Sicilian women, her dark, sultry beauty and acting talent ensured her stardom. Cardinale appeared in many famous Italian and French films in the 1960s and 1970s, as well as several English films, including *The Pink Panther* (1963), with David Niven, and the Sergio Leone Western, *Once Upon a Time in the West* (1968). She achieved international fame with her role in the Fellini classic, *8½* (1963), with Marcello Mastroianni. A passionate advocate for women's rights, Cardinale has served as a UNESCO goodwill ambassador for the Defense of Women's Rights since 2000.

# Leslie Caron

1931 ⌁ present

Franco-American actress and dancer Leslie Caron was born in the suburbs of Paris, France, and began her career as a ballerina in the Roland Petit Company. This is where Gene Kelly discovered Caron, casting her in *An American in Paris* (1951) to fill in for a pregnant Cyd Charisse. This led to an MGM contract and celebrated roles in *Lili* (1953) and *Gigi* (1958). Caron is one of the few to have danced with Fred Astaire, Gene Kelly, Mikhail Baryshnikov, and Rudolf Nureyev, and part of an exclusive group—including Rita Moreno, Margaret O'Brien, and June Lockhart—from the golden era of MGM musicals still active in film today. Most recently, Caron has played Countess Mavrodaki in the British TV series *The Durrells in Corfu* (2016).

# Cyd Charisse

## 1922 ∞ 2008

Born Tula Ellice Finklea in Amarillo, Texas, Cyd Charisse acquired the nickname "Sid" from her brother, when he tried to say "Sis." Producer Arthur Freed provided the more glamorous spelling of "Cyd" years later. To build up her strength after recovering from polio, she started ballet at age six; by twelve, she was studying ballet in Los Angeles; and by fourteen, she had joined the Ballet Russe de Monte Carlo. Charisse appeared as a ballerina in *Ziegfeld Follies* (1946), dancing with Fred Astaire. This led to her first speaking role in *The Harvey Girls* (1946), with Judy Garland. Known for her elegance and grace, Charisse was awarded the National Medal of the Arts and Humanities in 2006, the highest US honor for the arts.

# *Joan Crawford*

## 1905 ❧ 1977

Before her signature use of lipstick and shoulder pads, Joan Crawford started out as a chorus girl after winning a dancing contest. She moved to Hollywood and landed roles in silent films, successfully crossing over to sound with *Untamed* (1929), and becoming one of MGM's biggest stars in the 1930s. In 1945, her role in *Mildred Pierce* earned Crawford her only Academy Award for Best Actress. Married four times, Crawford adopted five children (one was reclaimed). It's said that her long-standing hatred of wire hangers—depicted in daughter Christina's *Mommie Dearest*—stems from a childhood job in a laundry. Her famous feud with Bette Davis added fire to their performances in *What Ever Happened to Baby Jane?* (1962), and more recently, was portrayed in the 2017 television series *Feud: Bette and Joan*.

# Dorothy Dandridge

## 1922 ✺ 1965

Dorothy Dandridge began her career singing with her sister Vivian in black Baptist churches before performing in the Cotton Club and the Apollo Theater. During the Depression, Dandridge moved to Los Angeles, where she hoped a bit part in *A Day at the Races* (1937) would be a stepping-stone. Unfortunately, for a black actress, roles were hard to come by, and she waited until 1940 before appearing in *Four Shall Die*. Despite facing discrimination and stereotypical roles, Dandridge was the first African-American woman to appear on the cover of *Life* magazine, and the first black actress to be nominated for a Best Actress Oscar, for her 1954 film, *Carmen Jones*. This award wouldn't be claimed by a black actress until Halle Berry won, in 2002.

# Bette Davis

## 1908 ∽ 1989

Often called the "First Lady of American Cinema," Bette Davis is known for her trademark delivery, her ever-present cigarette, and her utter fearlessness in portraying complicated characters with authenticity. Her breakthrough role came in *Of Human Bondage* (1934), and she won her first Oscar for *Dangerous* (1935). After fighting Warner Bros. for better roles, classic films like *Dark Victory* (1939) and *Now, Voyager* (1942) followed. Davis received her second Oscar nomination for *Jezebel* (1938), and in fact was nominated five years in a row, from 1939 through 1943. Her comeback performance in *All About Eve* (1950) contains one of the most-quoted lines in cinema history (think, fastening seat belts for a bumpy night). Married four times, her tempestuous personal life often mirrored the lives of her characters.

# Angie Dickinson

## 1931 ∽ present

Angie Dickinson originally dreamed of becoming a writer, inspired by her publisher father; instead, like many before her, she embarked on an acting career after winning a beauty contest. Her first big role was in *Gun the Man Down* (1956) with James Arness, and she starred opposite John Wayne and Dean Martin in 1959's *Rio Bravo*. Known for her blonde hair and voluptuous figure, for many years Dickinson insured her legs for $1 million (until the premiums got too expensive). She is perhaps best known for her role in *Police Woman* (1974–1978), for which she won a Golden Globe and three Emmys, and in recent years she has appeared in *Pay It Forward* (2000) and *Big Bad Love* (2001).

# Marlene Dietrich

## 1901 ↭ 1992

Marlene Dietrich, who held dual citizenship in Germany and America, began her career in Berlin, in theater and silent films. Her role as Lola-Lola in *The Blue Angel* (1930) caught the attention of Paramount, and she was soon starring in films like *Shanghai Express* (1932) and *Desire* (1936). Edith Head claimed the glamorous Dietrich knew more about fashion than any other actress. She not only became one of the most famous U.S. entertainers during World War II, she was also a humanitarian, providing financial assistance and housing for French and German exiles. Dietrich was extremely proud to receive the Medal of Freedom for her work in the war. In 1999, the American Film Institute named her the ninth greatest female star of classic Hollywood cinema.

# Deanna Durbin

## 1921 ⌒ 2013

Born Edna Mae Durbin, "Winnipeg's Sweetheart" had no idea that one day she would be the most highly paid female star in the world. Deanna Durbin's role in *Three Smart Girls* (1936) made her the darling of Hollywood, saving Universal Studios from bankruptcy. Deanna Durbin dolls and other merchandise flooded the market, and she was even considered for the role of Dorothy in *The Wizard of Oz* (1939). Durbin was Anne Frank's favorite movie star, earning her two spots on Anne's "Movie Wall" in the secret annex. A private person, Durbin struggled with her immense fame, and at the age of twenty-seven, she walked away from Hollywood to live a life of seclusion, eventually moving to France with her third husband.

# Barbara Eden

**1931     present**

Although she started out as a singer, Barbara Eden is best known for her role in *I Dream of Jeannie* (1965–1970). Matthew Broderick's dance sequence to the show's catchy theme song in *Ferris Bueller's Day Off* is perhaps one reason *People* magazine named Eden one of the greatest U.S. pop icons of the twentieth century. Eden has appeared in more than twenty films, including *Flaming Star* (1960) with Elvis Presley, and *The Brass Bottle* (1964), which led to Sidney Sheldon's *Jeannie* series. Eden has toured with shows like *The Sound of Music* (1965), and joined Bob Hope on a USO tour during the Persian Gulf War. She also volunteers with several charities, including the American Cancer Society and the Make-A-Wish Foundation.

# Britt Ekland

**1942 〜 present**

Born in Sweden, Britt Ekland personifies the beautiful Scandinavian blonde. After drama school and touring with a theater company, she pursued a career in cinema and became popular in Italy. A chance meeting with Peter Sellers led to romance and, just ten days later, marriage. Ekland appeared with Sellers in *After the Fox* (1966) and *The Bobo* (1967), but she's best known for her role in the British cult horror film *The Wicker Man* (1973), and as Bond girl Mary Goodnight in *The Man with the Golden Gun* (1974). One of the most photographed stars of the 1970s, Ekland had a highly publicized relationship with Rod Stewart. In later years she appeared in stage productions and independent films, and recently, Swedish reality TV shows.

# Jinx Falkenburg

## 1919 ⟨⟩ 2003

Nicknamed "Jinx" during childhood because her mother thought it would bring good luck, the moniker stuck. Jinx Falkenburg was discovered by fashion photographer Paul Hesse, and left school at sixteen to pursue modeling and acting. Her all-American, athletic beauty would grace the covers of more than two hundred magazines. While she appeared in several movies in the early 1940s, her real career began when she met "Tex" McCrary during an interview for a military publication. Although World War II interrupted their courtship, they were married after the war and soon hosted their own radio show. Falkenburg became a skilled interviewer, covering major stories of the day like the coronation of Queen Elizabeth II and the wedding of Grace Kelly to Prince Rainier.

# Alice Faye

## 1915 ∽ 1998

Alice Faye began her career as a singer with Rudy Vallee's band in the early 1930s, and got her first major break in *George White's 1935 Scandals*, when the lead dropped out. Darryl F. Zanuck helped change her image to a more-wholesome look for films like *Poor Little Rich Girl* (1936), starring Shirley Temple. In 1938, Faye teamed up with two of her fellow contract players, Tyrone Power and Don Ameche, in *In Old Chicago* (1938) and *Alexander's Ragtime Band* (1938), the latter one of the most successful musicals of the era. Although one of the top ten box-office draws in Hollywood by 1939, Faye left show business in 1945 to focus on her family, returning to make *State Fair* in 1952.

# Anne Francis

1930 ⤫ 2011

Anne Francis worked as a child model to help her family during the Great Depression, making her Broadway debut at age eleven. Her first starring role was in *Blackboard Jungle* (1955), followed by sci-fi classic *Forbidden Planet* (1956). She played a colorful PI in *Honey West* (1965–1966), the first TV series with a female detective's name in the title. The seductive Honey West had a black belt in judo and a pet ocelot named Bruce, and employed high-tech gadgets like tear-gas earrings to catch criminals, a la James Bond. Francis appeared in other popular series of the day, including *The Twilight Zone* and *Alfred Hitchcock Presents*, and in later years, episodes of *Dallas*, *Murder, She Wrote*, *Matlock*, and *The Golden Girls*.

# Zsa Zsa Gabor

## 1917 ∽ 2016

Known for her extravagant personality and lifestyle, Hungarian-American actress and socialite Zsa Zsa Gabor began her career in Vienna. She was much sought after in Hollywood for her "European flair and style," starring in 1950s films like *Moulin Rouge* (1952) and *Lovely to Look At* (1952). Gabor appeared regularly on television shows with Milton Berle, Johnny Carson, and Joan Rivers, and was a guest on Bob Hope specials and episodes of *The Dean Martin Celebrity Roast*. Gabor had a total of nine husbands, and once said, "I am a marvelous housekeeper. Every time I leave a man, I keep his house." After undergoing many legal, financial, and health difficulties, she died at the age of ninety-nine, just fifty days shy of becoming a centenarian.

# Greta Garbo

## 1905 ∽ 1990

Before Swedish-American actress Greta Garbo became famous, she worked as a "soap-latherer" in a Swedish barbershop. Impressed by her initial screen test, MGM producer Irving Thalberg took her under his wing, providing a weight-loss program, dental work, and English lessons. She began her career in silent films like *The Temptress* (1926), receiving rave reviews and becoming one of the biggest stars of the 1920s and 1930s. Her first role in a sound film was *Anna Christie* (1930), followed by *Mata Hari* (1931), *Grand Hotel* (1932), and *Camille* (1936), the latter considered her finest work, and Garbo's personal favorite. Nominated three times for Best Actress Oscar, she received an Honorary Award in 1954. Garbo retired from cinema at the age of thirty-five, shunning all publicity and leading a private life.

# *Ava Gardner*

## 1922 ∽ 1990

When Ava Gardner's brother-in-law exhibited her photo in his New York photography studio, MGM took notice and offered her a contract. Her first roles in the early 1940s were bit parts, often in B movies. Her true talent was revealed when she worked with directors like John Ford, in *Mogambo* (1953), for which she was nominated for an Oscar, and George Cukor, in *Bhowani Junction* (1956). Following her marriages with husbands Mickey Rooney, Artie Shaw, and Frank Sinatra, unhappy with Hollywood, she moved to Spain and made most of her next movies abroad. Her last quality leading role was in *The Night of the Iguana* (1964). She later relocated to England, where she spent the last twenty-two years of her life.

# Judy Garland

## 1922 ⤙⤚ 1969

Judy Garland remains one of the most beloved stars of any era. Born Frances Ethel Gumm in Minnesota, she was the youngest daughter of vaudevillians, and started singing onstage at the age of two. Although she would act in two dozen films with MGM, she is best remembered as Dorothy in *The Wizard of Oz* (1939). She often co-starred with Mickey Rooney and Gene Kelly, showcasing her enormous singing and dancing talent in *Meet Me in St. Louis* (1944) and *Easter Parade* (1948), and receiving Oscar nominations for *A Star Is Born* (1954) and *Judgment at Nuremberg* (1961). Although Garland achieved huge success in cinema, television, and the music industry, she struggled with addiction her whole life, dying tragically at the age of forty-seven from an accidental overdose.

# Paulette Goddard

### 1910 ∽ 1990

A child model, Paulette Goddard debuted in the Ziegfeld Follies at thirteen, becoming famous as "the girl on the crescent moon." One of twenty original Goldwyn Girls, along with Lucille Ball and Betty Grable, she met Charlie Chaplin in 1932. They became a couple, and he cast her in *Modern Times* (1936), and later, in *The Great Dictator* (1940). Goddard's fine work in *The Women* (1939), also starring Norma Shearer, Joan Crawford, and Rosalind Russell, earned her a contract with Paramount. She later married actor Burgess Meredith, appearing with him in *The Diary of a Chambermaid* (1946). Her popularity had faded by the late 1940s, and she left cinema to live in Europe, marrying German author Erich Maria Remarque in 1958.

# Betty Grable

## 1916 ⌘ 1973

Elizabeth Ruth Grable's mother was determined to make Betty a star, signing her up for dance lessons at age three, and taking her to Hollywood when she was twelve. Grable became a Goldwyn Girl, with bit parts in several 1930s films. Moviegoers finally paid attention when she took over for Alice Faye in *Down Argentine Way* (1940). She was photographed with her back to the camera in her famous pinup photo because she was pregnant at the time. This photo—which graced barracks worldwide during World War II—and roles in several successful musicals in the 1940s, made her the highest-paid star in Hollywood ($3 million per year, in today's currency). Sadly, Grable died of lung cancer at the young age of fifty-six.

# Jean Harlow

## 1911 ✦ 1937

Jean Harlow, the original blonde bombshell, ran away from home at sixteen to marry a businessman. They moved to Los Angeles, where Harlow landed small roles in several films in 1929. She divorced her husband after two years and concentrated on her career, getting her break in 1930 with Howard Hughes's *Hell's Angels*. As an MGM leading lady, she soon became more popular than colleagues Joan Crawford and Norma Shearer, packing theaters during a personal appearance tour on the East Coast in 1932. She would make six films with Clark Gable, including her last, *Saratoga* (1937), during which she was hospitalized. Her career was cut short when she died at the age of twenty-six from complications due to kidney failure.

# Rita Hayworth

### 1918 ❧ 1987

Born Margarita Carmen Cansino in Brooklyn, New York, Rita Hayworth planned to follow in her family's dancing footsteps. Noticed by a Fox studio head, she made her film debut at sixteen in *Dante's Inferno* (1935), followed by a series of small roles. She exploded into stardom after dancing with Fred Astaire in *You'll Never Get Rich* (1942), becoming one of the most beloved pinup girls of World War II. (Her picture was even glued to an A-bomb dropped on the Bikini Atoll during a 1946 test.) Playing the smoldering lead in *Gilda* (1946) opposite Glenn Ford made her a superstar. Hayworth was married five times, including to Orson Welles and Prince Aly Khan, making her the first movie star, before Grace Kelly, to marry a prince.

# Audrey Hepburn

## 1929 ∽ 1993

Audrey Hepburn and her mother were in the Netherlands in 1940, and when Hitler occupied the country, food shortages meant she had to resort to eating tulip bulbs to survive. Following liberation she went to ballet school and began modeling. Film producers came calling, and she appeared in films like *Roman Holiday* (1953), which earned her a Best Actress Oscar, *Sabrina* (1954), and *Funny Face* (1957). She was nominated for another Oscar for the role of Holly Golightly in *Breakfast at Tiffany's* (1961). Hubert de Givenchy, who designed her "little black dress" for this film, called Hepburn his muse. (In 2006, this dress sold at auction for more than $900,000.) Hepburn retired from acting in 1967, at the top of her game, and pursued humanitarian efforts as a UNICEF Goodwill Ambassador.

# Katharine Hepburn

## 1907 ⟋⟍ 2003

Katharine Hepburn was raised to be physically active and intellectually curious. She started acting at Bryn Mawr College, followed by small roles on Broadway. She entered the world of cinema in the 1930s, winning her first Academy Award for *Morning Glory* (1933). Audiences didn't know what to make of this quirky iconoclast who wore slacks, and no makeup. Once labeled "box-office poison," she regained her footing with the film version of *The Philadelphia Story* (1940) after making it a smash on Broadway. Teamed with Spencer Tracy for *Woman of the Year* (1942), their chemistry was palpable. Over the next twenty-five years they would appear together in eight more films. Hepburn had lost nothing of her magic when she appeared with Henry Fonda in *On Golden Pond* (1981), in her seventies.

# Grace Kelly

## 1929 ∾ 1982

Grace Kelly headed to New York right after high school to fulfill her dream of becoming an actress. Known for her work in Hitchcock films like *Dial M for Murder* (1954) and *Rear Window* (1954), she won an Oscar for her performance in *The Country Girl* (1954). In 1956 Kelly played her final role in *High Society*, after which she gave up her film career to marry Prince Rainier of Monaco. She would remain in the public eye until her untimely death in 1982. While driving back to Monaco from her country home, Kelly suffered a stroke, causing her to lose control of the car. The site of the accident is said to be where a picnic scene from her film *To Catch a Thief* (1955) was filmed, in 1954.

# Deborah Kerr

1921 ⌒ 2007

A shy child, Deborah Kerr found she could express her feelings through acting. After doing some stage work as a teenager, a British film producer cast Kerr in *Major Barbara* (1941) and *Love on the Dole* (1941). Kerr soon went to Hollywood, where she was cast as a proper English lady in a few films. She loved playing against type with Burt Lancaster in *From Here to Eternity* (1953), and then in 1957, she appeared in *An Affair to Remember* (1957), one of the most romantic films ever made. In 1968 she suddenly left movies, appalled by the sex and violence of the era. Kerr holds the record for most Oscar nominations for Best Actress without a win (six), redeemed when the Academy awarded her an Honorary Oscar in 1994.

# Veronica Lake

## 1922 ⌀ 1973

Veronica Lake's natural beauty and talent led her to Hollywood, where she enrolled in acting school. After appearing in the military drama *I Wanted Wings* (1940), Lake's popular peekaboo hairstyle was widely copied by her fans. When it became a hazard—"Rosie the Riveter" employees started getting their bangs caught in machinery—she participated in an awareness campaign to prevent injury. Lake received acclaim for *Sullivan's Travels* (1941) and for film noir roles with Alan Ladd, including *The Blue Dahlia* (1946). The intrepid actress took up flying, and in 1948 flew her small plane from LA to New York. Her career declined in the late 1940s, and she struggled with health issues until her early death at the age of fifty.

# Hedy Lamarr

## 1914 ❧ 2000

Born in Vienna, Hedy Lamarr is often considered the most beautiful woman to ever appear in films. After bit parts in German cinema, her fifth film, *Ecstasy* (1933), propelled her to stardom, largely because of her nude scene (which got it banned in the United States). Louis B. Mayer signed Lamarr to a contract nonetheless, and she soon appeared in exotic adventure films like *Algiers* (1938). She turned down roles in *Gaslight* (1940) and *Casablanca* (1942), appearing instead in *White Cargo* (1942) with Walter Pidgeon, which was a big success. Most of her roles emphasized her astonishing beauty without giving her many lines. Her career declined after the war, although she did appear in Cecil B. DeMille's epic *Samson and Delilah* (1949), which brought in $12 million.

# Janet Leigh

## 1927 ∽ 2004

When Norma Shearer saw Janet Leigh's photo, she believed the eighteen-year-old would be ideal for an MGM film that required a naive country girl. Shearer helped her to secure an MGM contract, and Leigh would go on to play ingenue roles with the likes of Errol Flynn, Gary Cooper, and James Stewart. Of her more than fifty films, Leigh is best remembered for her role in Hitchcock's *Psycho* (1960). The infamous shower scene—the filming of which required seven days—has entered public consciousness like few other big-screen moments. She would go on to appear in *The Manchurian Candidate* (1962) with Frank Sinatra, and then in made-for-TV movies. Leigh's daughter Jamie Lee Curtis would achieve fame for her similarly fright-inducing turn in *Halloween* (1978).

# Vivien Leigh

## 1913 ⟳ 1967

Fascinated by the first play she saw in London, Vivien Leigh enrolled in the Royal Academy of Dramatic Art, gradually landing small film roles. Her affair with Laurence Olivier while making *Fire Over England* (1937) coincided with her reading of *Gone with the Wind*. She asked her agent to recommend her for the role of Scarlett, and she was chosen over Norma Shearer, Katharine Hepburn, and Paulette Goddard, winning her first Oscar for this performance. (She would win a second years later for *A Streetcar Named Desire*, in 1951.) Leigh co-starred with Olivier in *21 Days Together* (1941) and *That Hamilton Woman* (1941), as well as *Romeo and Juliet*, on Broadway. Leigh struggled with health issues throughout her life, and died from chronic tuberculosis at fifty-three.

# Carole Lombard

## 1908 ⤬ 1942

Carole Lombard was playing baseball in the street when a director recruited her at the age of twelve. She signed a contract with Fox at sixteen, playing bit parts before moving on to larger roles in Westerns and comedies. In 1926 a car accident left her with a scarred face, repaired with plastic surgery. She got right back to work, making shorts for Mack Sennett in the late 1920s. Audiences loved her in the screwball comedies she was known for in the 1930s and 1940s, including *My Man Godfrey* (1936). Married to William Powell for two years, she later became the third wife of Clark Gable. Her bright career was cut short when she died in a plane crash, coming home from a war bond rally.

# Myrna Loy

## 1905 ◌ 1993

Myrna Loy spent her early years in Montana, trained as a dancer, and then began pursuing roles in silent films. One of her earliest experiences was as a chorus girl in *Pretty Ladies* (1925), along with Joan Crawford. After being cast as vamps or characters with Asian ancestry, Loy's career took off with her first appearance as Nora Charles in *The Thin Man* series (1934). Director W. S. Van Dyke had recognized her natural wit, used to wonderful effect opposite William Powell. She and Powell would appear in a total of fourteen films together—including *Libeled Lady* and *The Great Ziegfeld*, both in 1936—one of the most productive pairings in Hollywood history. Married four times, Loy died at the age of eighty-eight.

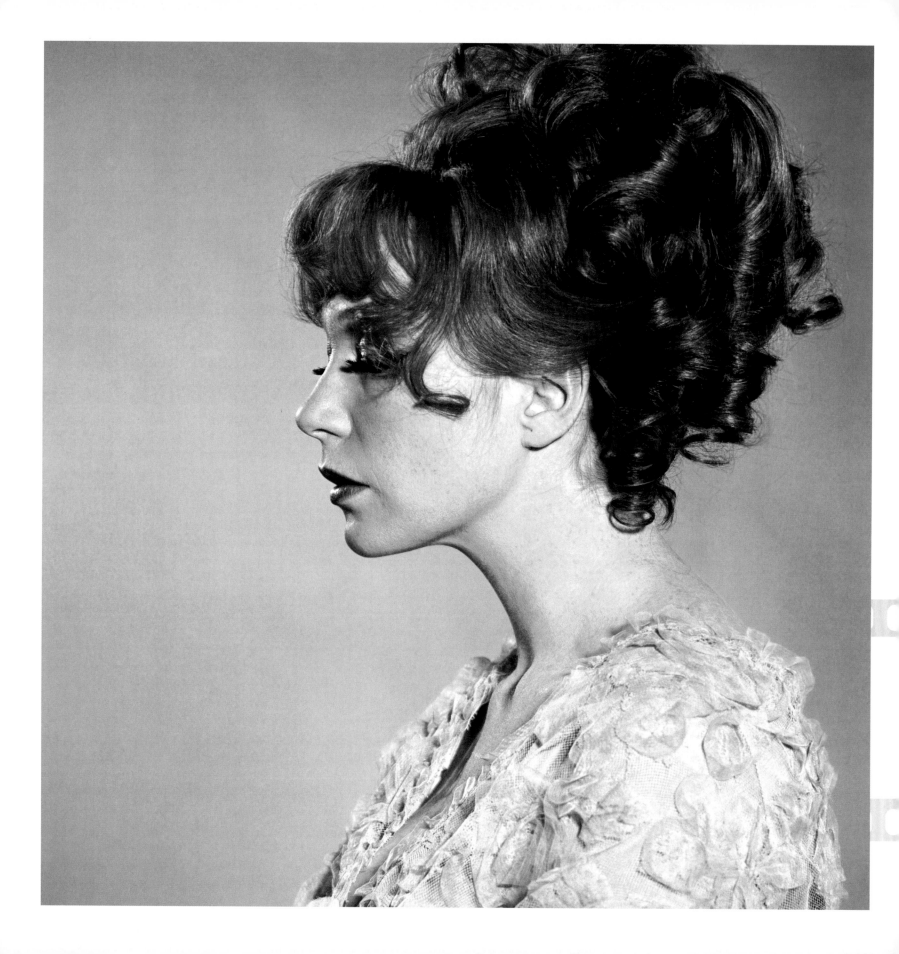

# Shirley MacLaine

## 1934 ∼ present

When understudy Shirley MacLaine took the stage in *The Pajama Game*, movie producer Hal B. Wallis happened to catch her performance. He signed her to a contract with Paramount, and MacLaine was off to shoot *The Trouble with Harry* (1955). Great roles followed, including *Some Came Running* (1958), *The Apartment* (1960), *Irma la Douce* (1963), and *The Turning Point* (1977), all of which led to Academy Award nominations. She finally won the Best Actress Oscar for her memorable turn in *Terms of Endearment* (1983). An actress, singer, dancer, activist, and author, MacLaine is also known for her interest in New Age spirituality, UFOs, and past lives. In recent years she appeared in the popular *Downton Abbey* series and the live-action *A Little Mermaid* (2018).

# Carmen Miranda

## 1909 ⌒ 1955

Born in Portugal, Carmen Miranda and her family moved to Brazil not long after she was born. Before she began wearing her trademark fruit hat, Miranda was a hat maker herself. After she became a popular singer in clubs and on the radio in Brazil, she was recruited for a Broadway show. Successful by the late 1930s, Miranda appeared in *Down Argentine Way* (1940) with Betty Grable and Don Ameche. Americans began adopting her style of dress, and a cartoon version of Miranda soon danced across movie screens prior to the main feature. After her film career, she continued on the nightclub circuit and on television. Brazil called for a period of national mourning when Miranda died of a heart attack at the age of forty-six.

# Pola Negri

1897 ⸻ 1987

After enduring poverty during her childhood in Poland, Pola Negri was accepted to the Imperial Ballet as a teen, later moving to the Warsaw Imperial Academy of Dramatic Arts. By seventeen she was starring onstage, until World War I brought abrupt changes to the theater scene. Negri shifted her focus to films and moved to Berlin, where she met German director Ernst Lubitsch. The success of *Madame DuBarry* (1919) brought them to Hollywood, where she continued to play femme fatales in *Forbidden Paradise* (1924) and *Hotel Imperial* (1927). Unfortunately, with the advent of sound, her career was hampered by her accent, as well as the censorship of the Hays Office codes. She returned to Europe, where she appeared in films for Pathé and UFA.

# Merle Oberon

## 1911 ∾ 1979

Born of Welsh and Indian parents, Merle Oberon spent her childhood in India. At seventeen she moved to London and worked as a club hostess, landing small roles in British films. When Hollywood beckoned, she left to try her luck in US films. Movie executives were impressed with her performance in *Vagabond Violinist* (1934), and her prestige grew when she was nominated for an Oscar for *The Dark Angel* (1935). To date, she is the only Asian actress to be nominated for a Best Actress Oscar. She appeared in several quality films over the years, but her most critically acclaimed performance was as Cathy Linton in *Wuthering Heights* (1939), opposite Laurence Olivier. Married four times, her last husband was twenty-five years her junior.

# Maureen O'Hara

## 1920 ❧ 2015

Maureen O'Hara was born in Ireland to a creative family. She had a natural gift for performing, and by fourteen had been accepted to the prestigious Abbey Theater, where she studied opera and classical theater. Charles Laughton was impressed with her screen test, and cast her in *Jamaica Inn* (1939). She went on to star in many classics, including *How Green Was My Valley* (1941), *Miracle on 34th Street* (1947), and *The Parent Trap* (1961), often playing proud, strong-willed Irish women. She starred in five films with John Wayne, the most beloved being *The Quiet Man* (1952), and worked with directors ranging from John Ford to Alfred Hitchcock. Her stunning beauty, lyric soprano voice, and athletic ability made her a versatile powerhouse.

# Debra Paget

**1933 ⌒ present**

Coming from a showbiz family, acting was always part of the plan for Debra Paget. Her mother helped her land a contract with 20th Century Fox by the age of fourteen, and her first role was in the film noir, *Cry of the City* (1948). Paget went on to appear in nearly twenty films at the studio, mostly swashbucklers, period musicals, and Westerns. Although she was only five-foot-two, she commanded the screen in Cecil B. DeMille's *The Ten Commandments* (1956), and in Elvis Presley's film debut, *Love Me Tender* (1956). Elvis fell in love with Paget during filming; however, she was in love with Howard Hughes at the time, so nothing came of the romance. Paget married a Chinese millionaire in 1962 and retired from her film career.

# Lilli Palmer

## 1914 ∽ 1986

Lilli Palmer, born in Prussia to Jewish parents, studied drama and made her onstage debut in Berlin, in 1932. The family fled to Paris during Hitler's rise to power, and Palmer later moved to England, appearing in *Crime Unlimited* (1935), and Alfred Hitchcock's *Secret Agent* (1936). Her life changed when she married Rex Harrison in 1943. They moved to the United States in 1945, acting together in films and on the Broadway stage. Palmer also co-starred with other leading actors of the day, like Gary Cooper and John Garfield, before leaving Harrison—and Hollywood—to return to Europe in 1954. She would appear in European productions for the rest of her life, mostly German and French, although she did make a few more movies in Hollywood.

# Mary Pickford

## 1892 ⌘ 1979

Born in Toronto, Mary Pickford began her career at the age of seven, touring with her family in a number of theater companies. Arguably the silent era's most renowned female star, Pickford was a trailblazer. She co-founded United Artists film studio with Douglas Fairbanks, Charlie Chaplin, and D. W. Griffith, and was one of the thirty-six founders of the Academy of Motion Picture Arts and Sciences. She was also one of the earliest stars to be billed under her own name, in films like *My Best Girl* (1927). She earned the nickname "Queen of the Movies" in the 1910s and 1920s, and was awarded the second-ever Best Actress Oscar for *Coquette* (1929). She turned down the role of Norma Desmond in *Sunset Boulevard* (1950), which went to Gloria Swanson.

# Ginger Rogers

## 1911 ⌒ 1995

Born Virginia Katherine McMath in Independence, Missouri, Ginger Rogers and her family moved to Texas when she was nine. After winning a Charleston dance contest in 1925, she launched a vaudeville career, followed by Broadway and a contract with Paramount. Ginger Rogers appeared in ten films with Fred Astaire, including *Top Hat* (1935), *Swing Time* (1936), *Shall We Dance* (1937), and *The Barkleys of Broadway* (1949), before branching out into comedies and dramatic roles. She was one of the biggest draws in the 1940s, winning the Best Actress Oscar for her performance in *Kitty Foyle* (1940). By the end of the 1940s her popularity began to wane. She returned to Broadway and other traveling theater productions in the 1960s, retiring in 1984.

# Jane Russell

## 1921 ～ 2011

One of the most famous sex symbols in Hollywood in the 1940s and 1950s, Jane Russell studied acting at Max Reinhardt's Theatrical Workshop, and with Maria Ouspenskaya. She signed a contract with Howard Hughes for *The Outlaw* (1943), her role designed to show off her voluptuous figure. This film garnered a lot of attention, and made her a popular pinup girl with servicemen during World War II. Bob Hope, her favorite co-star—she was Calamity Jane to his Peter Potter in *The Paleface* (1948)—often praised her physical attributes. She had similar roles in films like *His Kind of Woman* (1951) and *The Las Vegas Story* (1952), although she's best known for the hugely successful *Gentlemen Prefer Blondes* (1953), opposite Marilyn Monroe.

# Eva Marie Saint

## 1924 ∽ present

In a career that has spanned seventy years, Eva Marie Saint is perhaps best known for her starring role in Elia Kazan's *On the Waterfront* (1954), for which she won a Best Supporting Actress Oscar, and Alfred Hitchcock's *North by Northwest* (1959). Born in New Jersey, Saint studied acting at Bowling Green State University. Her early career began in radio and television, and in 1953 she won the Drama Critics Award for her Broadway stage role in *The Trip to Bountiful*, co-starring with such luminaries as Lillian Gish and Jo Van Fleet. She was married for sixty-five years to producer and director Jeffrey Hayden—a rare accomplishment in Hollywood—until his death in 2016 at the age of ninety.

# Norma Shearer

## 1902 ⌘ 1983

After seeing a vaudeville show one day, Norma Shearer announced she would be an actress—this, in spite of her less-than-ideal figure and crossed eyes. (She would visit eye doctors and do muscle-strengthening exercises throughout her career.) Shearer moved to New York in 1920 and charmed her way into being an extra at Universal Pictures. Other bit parts followed, including one directed by D. W. Griffith. After repeated rejections, the determined Shearer impressed Irving Thalberg enough that he cast her in *He Who Gets Slapped* in 1924—and married her in 1927. She became a star, making thirteen silent films for MGM by 1927. Her first sound film was *The Trial of Mary Dugan* (1929), and she would win an Oscar for *The Divorcee* (1930).

# Ann Sheridan

## 1915 ❧ 1967

Born in Texas, Ann Sheridan was active in drama during high school and college. When she won a beauty contest—the prize, a bit part in the Paramount film, *The Search for Beauty* (1934)—Sheridan left college to pursue a Hollywood career. Her first leading role was in *Car 99* (1935) with Fred MacMurray. B picture stardom followed, with Warner Bros. finally taking notice after her supporting role in *Letter of Introduction* (1938), and her performance in *Angels with Dirty Faces* (1938), with James Cagney and Humphrey Bogart. In 1939 Warner Bros. announced that Sheridan had been voted the actress with the most "oomph" in America. A popular pinup girl in the early 1940s, she once received 250 marriage proposals in a single week.

# Barbara Stanwyck

1907 ∽ 1990

Born in Brooklyn, New York, Barbara Stanwyck cherished a longtime dream of a career in show business. When she wasn't working at the telephone company, she was looking for dancing jobs. Eventually hired as a chorus girl for forty dollars a week, she was determined to make the most of the opportunity. She moved to Hollywood in 1928 and proved to be versatile in all genres, from melodramas like *Stella Dallas*, in 1937, to thrillers like *Double Indemnity* (1944). She excelled equally in comedies and Westerns, especially her last and most memorable role in TV's *The Big Valley* (1965). Nominated for four Academy Awards (she never won), she worked hard at her craft, and was considered a pleasure to have on set because of her easygoing personality.

# *Gloria Stuart*

## 1910 ⌒ 2010

Gloria Stuart probably never imagined she would live to be a hundred, much less appear in one of the highest-grossing films of all time, *Titanic* (1997). She began by acting in her senior class play, and then at the University of California at Berkeley. After seeing her in a production of *The Seagull*, two talent scouts fought over her, famously flipping a coin; Universal won. She appeared in *The Invisible Man* (1933) and *Roman Scandals* (1933), along with films for other studios, before leaving the cinema and seeking roles onstage in New York. In later years, she expressed her creativity by opening an art furniture shop, taking up oil painting, and learning the craft of fine printing. The Academy honored her with a centennial celebration in 2010.

# Gloria Swanson

## 1899 ⌒ 1983

Destined to be one of the greatest stars of the silent film era, Gloria Swanson never intended to go into show business. At eighteen, on a movie studio tour, she was picked out of the crowd to be an extra. Other small roles followed, and after meeting her first husband on set, they moved to Los Angeles, where she appeared in films like *The Pullman Bride* (1917) and *Don't Change Your Husband* (1919). (Swanson wouldn't follow that advice, going on to have six more husbands.) The highest-paid actress in Hollywood by the mid-1920s, she adapted well to sound. She would achieve a smash hit with *Sunset Boulevard* (1950), where she uttered one of the most iconic lines in film history: "All right, Mr. DeMille, I'm ready for my close-up."

# Sharon Tate

Before becoming one of the most famous victims of mass murder, Sharon Tate grew up in a military family that was stationed in various cities. She won several beauty contests, and her stunning looks and charm led to a role as an extra in a movie shot in Italy. Commercials and modeling gigs followed, and eventually, a role on *The Beverly Hillbillies* (1962). Tate met future husband Roman Polanski on the set of *The Fearless Vampire Killers* (1967), and would play a starlet in *Valley of the Dolls* that same year. Tate traveled in the rarefied air of the Hollywood circle, meeting influential cinema leaders. Who knows what she might have achieved if members of the Manson family hadn't shown up at her home on August 9, 1969.

# Elizabeth Taylor

## 1932 ∽ 2011

One of the last big stars to come through the old Hollywood studio system, Elizabeth Taylor lived in London until 1939, when the looming world war led her family to move to Los Angeles. After earning a contract with Universal, Taylor appeared in classics like *Lassie Come Home* (1943) and *National Velvet* (1944), opposite Mickey Rooney. Roles in *Life with Father* (1947) and *Little Women* (1949) followed, and she would earn Oscars for *BUtterfield 8* (1960) and *Who's Afraid of Virginia Woolf?* (1966). Known for her love of the finer things, including jewelry, Taylor was married eight times—twice to Richard Burton, whom she met while filming the blockbuster, *Cleopatra* (1963). In later years Taylor worked tirelessly on behalf of AIDS patients, raising more than $270 million for the cause.

# Shirley Temple

## 1928 ❦ 2014

Certainly the most celebrated child star of all time, Shirley Temple entered show business at three; by five, she had made *Bright Eyes* (1934). Moviegoers flocked to theaters throughout the Great Depression to see the cheerful star in films like *Curly Top* (1935), *Heidi* (1937), and *Rebecca of Sunnybrook Farm* (1938), making her the biggest box-office draw for this period. A talented actor and singer—known for classic songs like "On the Good Ship Lollipop" and "Animal Crackers in My Soup"—she was also a brilliant dancer, able to keep up with Bill "Bojangles" Robinson. At age six she became the first recipient of the juvenile Academy Award, the youngest ever to receive one. After her film career, she served as a US ambassador to Ghana and Czechoslovakia.

# Thelma Todd

Thelma Todd had planned to become a schoolteacher, but a local beauty contest title led her to enter the Miss America pageant. Although she didn't win, talent scouts liked what they saw. She appeared in some comedy shorts for Hal Roach, and signed to Paramount. After *Fascinating Youth* (1926), she starred with Gary Cooper and William Powell in *Nevada* (1927). She made twenty films in 1928 and 1929 alone. Successfully transitioning to sound films, she employed her comedic gifts throughout the early 1930s, appearing in Marx Brothers films like *Monkey Business* (1931) and *Horse Feathers* (1932). She also joined Cary Grant in his first movie, *This Is the Night* (1932). Her tragic death at twenty-nine was ruled a suicide, but remains a mystery today.

# Lana Turner

Lana Turner's talent far surpassed her MGM nickname of "Sweater Girl." After her father's death in 1929, her mother moved the family to California, where Turner entered the world of cinema at seventeen. Bit parts led to a role in *Love Finds Andy Hardy* (1938), with Mickey Rooney. Her alluring beauty made hearts flutter, and by the 1940s Turner was a major star for MGM, appearing in films like *Ziegfeld Girl* (1941) and *Dr. Jekyll and Mr. Hyde* (1941), as well as her brilliant turn in *The Postman Always Rings Twice* (1946). Married eight times, Turner had a tumultuous private life, which didn't stop her from later success in *Imitation of Life* (1959), and roles on the small screen, like *Falcon Crest* (1982–1983), her loveliness still intact.

# Mamie Van Doren

## 1931 ∾ present

Born in South Dakota, Mamie Van Doren and her family moved to Los Angeles in 1942. She worked as an usher at a movie theater and had a bit part in an early TV series before signing a contract with Universal in 1953. Her first major role that same year was in *The All American*, with Tony Curtis. The studio had high hopes she would achieve the same superstar status as Marilyn Monroe (at the time, Van Doren, Marilyn Monroe, and Jayne Mansfield were known as "The Three M's"). Although this didn't happen, Van Doren appeared in many films that have gained a cult following over the years, including the rock 'n' roll movie *Untamed Youth* (1957), later featured in an episode of *Mystery Science Theater 3000*.

# Anna May Wong

## 1905 ⚬ 1961

Anna May Wong was the first Chinese-American actress to gain worldwide recognition, her career spanning silent and sound film, television, stage, and radio. Born to second-generation Chinese-American parents, Wong fell in love with the cinema. In the silent era, she appeared in Douglas Fairbanks's swashbuckler, *The Thief of Bagdad* (1924); later, she joined Marlene Dietrich in *Shanghai Express* (1932), becoming a fashion icon and achieving international stardom for her film and stage work. In 1935, MGM refused to consider her for the lead in *The Good Earth*, choosing a white actress instead. She went on to portray Chinese and Chinese Americans in a positive light in the late 1930s, scaling back her film work during World War II to help the Chinese cause against Japan.

# Natalie Wood

## 1938 ~ 1981

Born of Russian immigrant parents, Natalie Wood appeared in more than twenty films during her childhood, winning the hearts of moviegoers in *Miracle on 34th Street* (1947). Wood had continued success as a young adult, earning three Oscar nominations before the age of twenty-five. As a teen, she was nominated for Best Supporting Actress Oscar for *Rebel Without a Cause* (1955). She starred in *West Side Story* (1961) and *Gypsy* (1962), and received Best Actress Oscar nominations for *Splendor in the Grass* (1961) and *Love with the Proper Stranger* (1963). Her relationship with Robert Wagner was thrust into the spotlight when she drowned at the age of forty-three while aboard his yacht, *Splendour*, in 1981. Decades later, the circumstances of her death still incite controversy and suspicion.

# Fay Wray

## 1907 ❧ 2004

Canadian-American actress Fay Wray is best known for playing Ann Darrow in the 1933 film, *King Kong*. Dubbed one of the first "scream queens," Wray became internationally famous for her roles in horror films in a career that spanned nearly sixty years. She started out with Paramount as a teenager, and then moved on to other studios. After a brief retirement in the 1940s, financial pressures led her to return to acting. Wray appeared in a variety of films, and later, on the small screen as well, including episodes of *Perry Mason* and *Alfred Hitchcock Presents* in the 1950s, and other series and television movies in the 1960s. James Cameron approached her to play the part of Old Rose in *Titanic*, but she turned it down.

# Loretta Young

## 1913 ⤠ 2000

Beginning as a child actor in the silent-film era, Loretta Young appeared with Lon Chaney in MGM's *Laugh, Clown, Laugh* (1928), and co-starred with Clark Gable in the 1935 film version of *The Call of the Wild*. During World War II, Young appeared in *Ladies Courageous* (1944), the fictionalized story of the Women's Auxiliary Ferrying Squadron, a group of female pilots who flew bomber planes from factories to their final destinations. In 1947 she won an Oscar for her role in *The Farmer's Daughter*, her best-remembered film. From the 1950s into 1961, Young hosted and starred in an anthology TV series, *The Loretta Young Show.* This became the longest-running prime-time network show hosted by a woman up to that time, and won three Emmy Awards.

# About the Author

**Melissa J. Hayes** is the author of *A Mug-up with Elisabeth,* a companion for readers of Maine author Elisabeth Ogilvie, and has edited books ranging from *Small Miracles of the Holocaust* to *Brothers in Valor,* battlefield stories of African-American Medal of Honor recipients. She has a passion for classical Hollywood cinema, particularly films from the 1940s. She lives in Connecticut.